What's the difference between mononucleosis and herpes?
You get mono by snatching a kiss.

◆

What's brown and sits on a piano bench?
Beethoven's first movement.

◆

What do you call a child raised in a house of ill repute?
A brothel sprout.

◆

Did you hear what happened to the man who had sex with his canary?
He got twerpies, and the worst thing is that it's untweetable.

◆

How does a Jewish couple perform "doggie style" sex?
He sits up and begs and she lays down and plays dead.

◆

What do senators use instead of bookmarks?
Bent-over pages.

TURN THE PAGE FOR MORE
OUTRAGEOUSLY OFFENSIVE JOKES!

Outrageously OFFENSIVE JOKES

MAUDE THICKETT

PUBLISHED BY POCKET BOOKS NEW YORK

This book is a work of fiction. Names, characters, places and incidents are either the product of the author's imagination or are used fictitiously. Any resemblance to actual events or locales or persons, living or dead, is entirely coincidental.

Another *Original* publication of POCKET BOOKS

POCKET BOOKS, a division of Simon & Schuster, Inc.
1230 Avenue of the Americas, New York, N.Y. 10020

ISBN: 0-671-49633-6

First Pocket Books printing August, 1983

10 9 8 7 6 5

Printed in the U.S.A.

For Joseph and Rosemarie
and their "son" Baron

Acknowledgments

I would like to thank the many people who have contributed to the making of this book. Many will remain nameless to protect their reputations, but there are a few brave souls who don't give a damn. Although not completely identified, they are as follows:

Many thanks to Stuart M., Jim 7, Scott A., Debbie S., Brian B., Dave T., Vinnie V., Sandy R., Trish B., Bill G., Candice L., JoAnn V., Yolanda I., Charlotte W., all my friends at S&S, and the editorial staff at Pocket Books.

Also, thanks to Terry R. at Key West Island Books, Mike G., Gloria L., and Beth R. from Western Merchandisers, Jane G. and the gang at Pic-A-Book, Allan W., Rene G., Tim G., and Keith G. of Waghalter's, and all of my other bookstore friends who have pitched in.

My thanks also go to the gang at "the show," along with Dom and Grace G., Jim and Rose C., Jimmy "the Weed" C., Betty T. and family, Bob P., Nancy B., and Robin S., Richard and Bev S. And my deepest gratitude to Uncle Dutch—he had a million of 'em.

Contents

Celebrities

How can you identify Dolly Parton's kids at a party?

They're the ones with stretch marks around their mouths.

♦

How did Helen Keller burn her face?

Bobbing for french fries.

♦

Why was Lady Di disappointed on her honeymoon?

She thought that all rulers had twelve inches.

♦

Why does Don Meredith have so many children?

He uses flow-through tea bags.

♦

What do you get when you cross a black man with Bo Derek?

The ten of spades.

♦

How did Helen Keller's parents punish her?

They left the plunger in the toilet bowl.

♦

President Reagan was flying back to the U.S. after special talks with Cuban leaders. As his helicopter passed over the Florida Everglades, he spotted two white men in a speedboat, dragging a black man behind them on a rope.

Reagan asked the pilot to bring the chopper down alongside the boat. Once in hearing range, Reagan turned on the microphone and yelled, "I sure do think it's wonderful of you two boys to take a black man water-skiing. It's refreshing to see that there isn't any prejudice in Florida."

As the helicopter flew off, one of the boaters turned to the other and said, "He may be president of the whole fucking country, but he sure don't know shit about huntin' alligator."

♦

Where did Prince Charles spend his honeymoon?

In-Diana.

♦

What's black and white and has three eyes?

Sammy Davis Jr. and his ex-wife.

♦

A woman walks into a tattoo parlor.
"Do you do custom work?" she asks the artist.
"Why of course!"
"Good. I'd like a portrait of Robert Redford on the inside of my right thigh, and a portrait of Paul Newman on the inside of my left thigh."
"No problem," says the artist. "Strip from the waist down and get up on the table."
After two hours of hard work, the artist finishes. The woman sits up and examines the tattoos.
"That doesn't look like them!" she complains loudly.
"Oh yes it does," the artist says indignantly, "and I can prove it." With that, he runs out of the shop and grabs the first man off the street he can find; it happens to be the town drunk.
"Well, what do you think?" the woman asks, spreading her legs. "Do you know who these men are?"
The drunk studies the tattoos for a couple of minutes and says. "I'm not sure who the guys on either side are, but the fellow in the middle is definitely Willie Nelson!"

◆

Why did Helen Keller have a sheltered childhood?

Because her parents always kept her in the dark.

◆

What is Helen Keller's least favorite television show?

The Wonderful World of Color.

♦

What part of Popeye never rusts?

The part he puts in Olive Oyl.

♦

What do Linda Lovelace and the Bermuda Triangle have in common?

They both swallow seamen.

♦

Why did Idi Amin kill 5,000 people?

To keep up with the Joneses.

♦

What's Margaret Thatcher's favorite song?

Don't Falk with me, Argentina.

♦

Queen Elizabeth and Princess Di were being driven in the royal Rolls to a gala affair at a country estate. They were, of course, dressed and jeweled to the teeth.

While traveling the back country roads they were stopped by a masked, armed bandit who ordered them and their driver out of the car.

"All right, Queen Elizabeth, hand over your valuables," the bandit demanded.

"My good man," she replied, "don't be ridiculous. Do you think I'd travel with my jewels, unguarded?"

"All right then, Di," he said, turning to the princess, "let's have yours then."

"Don't be absurd," she replied, "I don't even walk the palace garden with my engagement ring!"

Angry and frustrated, the bandit consoled himself by driving off with the royal car. As he drove away in a cloud of dust, the queen turned to Di and said, "I'm so glad we had time to hide the jewels in our own private places."

"Yes," the princess replied. "He never thought to look up our twats."

"It's a pity Margaret didn't come along," her mother-in-law said, "we could have saved the Rolls, too!"

♦

How did Helen Keller's mother torment her?

She put doorknobs on all the walls.

♦

Why can't you go to the bathroom at a Beatles' concert?

There's no john.

Hey, Leroy!

Why don't blacks drive convertibles?

Their lips would flap them to death.

♦

Have you heard about the new civil service test the city of Chicago is using since they elected a black mayor?

Applicants must run the 100-yard dash while carrying a TV set.

♦

Did you hear about Klu Klux Knievel?

He tried to jump over eight black men with a steamroller.

♦

Why did the black man wear a tuxedo to his vasectomy?

If he was going to *be* impotent he wanted to *look* impotent.

♦

The body of a black civil liberties worker, which was wrapped in chains, was pulled out of a lake in the deep South. The local newspaper reporter asked the sheriff for his thoughts on the case. The sheriff replied, "Shoot! Ain't that just like a black boy, stealing more chains than he could swim with."

◆

Why do black men like to wear high-heeled shoes?

To keep from scraping their knuckles when they walk.

◆

What do you call a black man in court?

Guilty.

◆

What's long and hard on a black man?

Second grade.

◆

Why aren't there more black astronauts?

Because their lips explode at 75,000 feet.

◆

How do you get a black man out of a tree in Alabama?

Cut the rope.

◆

Did you hear about the plan to rid the country of Puerto Ricans?

They're going to tell the blacks that they taste like southern fried chicken.

♦

What's black and brown and looks good on a black man?

A Doberman.

♦

Did you hear about the black man who insisted he was Hispanic?

He gave himself away when he said, "Adios, motherfucker."

♦

How do you stop five black men from raping a woman?

Throw them a basketball.

♦

Do you know what they call the Harlem branch of Toys 'R Us?

WeBeToys.

♦

Did you hear about the new sign they erected

over Chicago's Cook County jail when the black mayor took office?

It says "Washington slept here."

◆

How do you save a drowning black man?

Throw him an anchor.

◆

Two black women were talking about their sex lives.

One woman turns to the other and says, "Do you and your husband have mutual orgasms?"

"No," answers her friend. "We have State Farm."

◆

How did South Carolina blacktop its highways?

They lined up two black families and ran over them with steamrollers.

◆

Why do blacks wear wide-brimmed hats?

It keeps the pigeon shit off their lips.

◆

What do the Kinney Shoe Corporation and the Post Office have in common?

30,000 black loafers.

◆

What do you call a black man mixing cement with a pitchfork?

A mortar forker.

◆

Why do blacks always have sex on their minds?

Because they have pubic hair on their heads.

◆

A black woman was washing her clothes in a pasture stream. She was leaning over a scrub board, her skirt tied up so it wouldn't get wet; her devil red panties were showing.

A bull in the pasture caught sight of the panties and charged. WHAM! The woman kept on with her wash, and said calmly, "I don't know who you is and I don't know where you come from, but I'm here every Monday, Wednesday, and Friday!"

◆

Why don't they allow blacks to swim in the Hudson River?

Because they leave a ring.

◆

What do you call a black prostitute with braces?

A Black & Decker pecker wrecker.

◆

Why don't more black women become nuns?

They can't remember to say "Superior" after "Mother."

◆

What's black foreplay?

"Wake up, bitch."

◆

Did you hear about the new war movie in production with an all-black cast?

A Pack of Lips, Now.

◆

What do you call ten black men on a white guy?

A fair fight.

◆

Did you see the two blacks on "That's Incredible"?

One had a job and the other knew who his father was.

What's black and yellow and screams?

A bus full of black kids going off a cliff.

Two blacks are promoted to sergeant. They decide to celebrate by going into town and getting laid. After they find a prostitute they both like they follow her back to her room. As they're getting undressed, she says, "Look, I want to be honest with you; I have gonorrhea."

Neither man knows what gonorrhea is, so one goes to get a dictionary and look it up. He returns a few minutes later and says, "No problem. Let's get on with it!"

A few weeks later, both men start to burn and discharge. They go to the camp doctor who informs them that they both have the clap.

"I thought you looked that word up," says the first man.

"I did, and I could have sworn we were safe!"

"Why? What did it say?"

"It said 'Gonorrhea: a disease of the privates.'"

What's this?

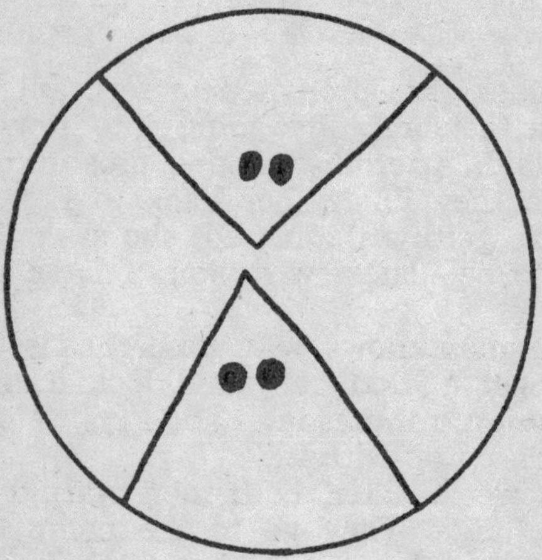

The last thing a black man sees after being thrown into a well.

◆

Why do blacks make such good hurdlers?

They're raised jumping turnstiles.

◆

Otto and his pet gorilla walked into a bar. The bartender demanded that Otto leave the premises, since pets—especially big ones—were not allowed. Otto promised, however, that they'd make no trouble, and he and his pet were allowed to go into the back room for one drink only.

Five minutes after Otto got his drink, a drunk in the main barroom began to panhandle for money. The drunk spied Otto in the back room, and decided to approach him. Having had no luck with Otto, the drunk turned to the gorilla and said drunkenly, "How about you, boy?"

When the gorilla didn't respond, Otto tried to intervene, but the drunk became violent. Seeing his master being attacked, the gorilla grabbed the drunk and flung him across the room, where he crashed into a wall.

The bartender rushed in, yelling, "I told you people I didn't want trouble in here!"

The drunk shaking his head to clear it, said, "No trouble here. It's just when you give a nigger a fur coat he thinks he owns the world!"

Maladies

Did you hear about the guy who lost his whole left side in an accident?

He's all right.

♦

How did herpes leave the hospital?

On crotches.

♦

The doctor went into his patient's room and said, "I've got some good news and some bad news. Which do you want to hear first?"

"The bad news," said the frightened patient.

"During your hernia operation the resident's knife slipped, and cut off your penis."

"My God! Then what's the good news?"

"It wasn't malignant."

♦

How did the leper stop the card game?

He threw his hand in.

♦

What's the hardest part of a vegetable to eat?

The wheelchair.

◆

How did Captain Hook meet his death?

Jock itch.

◆

An old man went to the doctor.

"Doctor, you've got to help me. Every morning at six o'clock I have to pass water and move my bowels."

"So what's wrong with that?"

"You don't understand! I don't get up until nine o'clock!"

◆

The captain went to his sergeant and said, "We need a very special man for a very dangerous mission. He must be extraordinarily brave, highly dependable, and have nerves of steel. Think about it tonight; we can talk in the morning about who you feel is the right man for the job."

"I don't need the time, sir," the sergeant said. "I already know that Private Jones is our man."

"What makes you so sure?"

"Because last week while we were showing the men the training film on VD, he ate strawberry shortcake through the whole damn movie."

◆

What's the difference between mononucleosis and herpes?

You get mono by snatching a kiss.

♦

Did you hear what happened to the man who had sex with his canary?

He got twerpies, and the worst thing is that it's untweetable.

♦

Mr. Stern hadn't been feeling very well lately, so his loving wife made an appointment for him with their family doctor. She asked the doctor to let her know immediately if the prognosis was unfavorable; she would break the news to her husband gently.

Later that day, the doctor phoned. It was very bad; as a matter of fact it was much worse than he originally thought—her husband had less than twenty-four hours to live. The only blessing was that when he went, it would be quick and painless.

Mrs. Stern decided that this last night would be the most wonderful night of her husband's life. She prepared his favorite meal and met him at the door with his favorite cocktail in hand. After an exquisite meal, they retired to the darkened bedroom for after-dinner drinks. Mrs. Stern put on her sexiest nightgown and perfume and approached her husband. "Whatever you want to do, whatever fantasies you have, tonight is the night to fulfill them."

They made wild, passionate love. "That was great," said Mr. Stern. "Let's do it again." So they did, and he said, "That was even better. Let's do it again!"

"That's easy for you to say," said his wife. "You don't have to get up in the morning."

♦

Did you hear about the queer deaf-mute?

Neither did he.

♦

What happened when the butcher backed into his meat grinder?

He got a little behind in his orders.

♦

A woman is undressing in front of her husband on their wedding night. He notices that the nipple of her left breast is located on the side of the breast. Then he sees that her navel is off-center, almost all the way over on her left hip. Unable to hide his surprise and revulsion, he exclaims, "Boy, are you built strange!"

Naturally offended, his bride lifts her arm, points to her armpit and says, "Yeah? Well you can kiss my ass!"

♦

What's the difference between love and herpes?

Herpes is forever.

♦

Ask a leper for an inch and he'll give you a foot.

♦

Why did they have to call off the lepers' hockey game?

There was a face off in the corner.

♦

Did you hear about the man who had five pricks?

His pants fit him like a glove.

♦

The Hunchback of Notre Dame wanted to go on vacation. He asked the bishop for some time off.

"But who will ring the bell?" asked the bishop.

"I don't know," replied Quasimodo. "All I know is that I really need a vacation. Why don't you find a temporary replacement?"

So the bishop put up a help wanted sign outside the cathedral. No one, it seemed, was interested in ringing the bell for a week or two while Quasimodo was on vacation. On the day before Quasimodo was due to leave for the south of France, two men walked into the bishop's office. They were identical except for the fact that one of the men had no arms.

"I'd like to ring the bell while Quasimodo is on vacation," said the man with arms. "My brother here will be taking over for me on Sundays; I go to church at Chartres."

The bishop was desperate for a replacement so he agreed to let the man give it a try. He took the brothers to the top of the bell tower. The first brother grabbed the rope and pulled it hard. Off went the bell—a beautiful, clear ring. Excited, the man ran over to embrace his brother. "We've got the job!" he yelled. In his excitement, however, the man bumped the guard rail which, being old, gave way. The bishop heard a sickening thud as the man hit the ground.

"Well, I guess I'd better give it a try," said the armless brother.

"Be serious," said the bishop. "You can't possibly ring that bell."

"Listen, your Holiness. You should at least give me a chance. Look at it this way: It's your last chance to find a replacement for Quasimodo."

The bishop agreed reluctantly, and the armless man took a good running start, flinging himself at the famous bell. He hit it face first, and the huge bell swung loudly. Unfortunately, the force of the swinging bell knocked the man off the top of the bell tower. The bishop beard another thud, and ran to get a doctor.

When the doctor arrived, he did a quick examination of both men. He pronounced the first man dead, and the armless man alive, but unconscious.

"Who is this man?" asked the doctor, pointing to the armless man.

"I don't know," said the bishop, "but his face sure rings a bell."

"And who's the other guy?" the doctor queried.

"Don't know that either," replied the bishop. "But he's a dead ringer for his brother."

Goldstein, Goldman, and Goldberg

What's the object of a Jewish football game?

To get the quarter back.

◆

A JAP went to the gynecologist for the first time. She undressed, got up onto the examining table and put her feet in the stirrups. The doctor began his examination and said, "This is the biggest vagina I've ever seen!"

"Well you didn't have to say it twice!" she said, insulted.

"I didn't," he replied.

◆

Maxie was going down on Becky, when she farted.

Maxie looked up. "Thank God!" he said. "A breath of fresh air!"

◆

Sadie Feingold was on safari. She was taking pictures when a huge gorilla swung down out of a tree and carried her off to his lair, where he used and abused her in ways she had never even heard about. Luckily, a rescue party found her while her captor was in search of a banana, and took her back to civilization. While she was recuperating in the hospital, her best friend came to visit. "Sadie! Such a terrible experience, but at least you're alive." Sadie was silent. "Sadie! Say something!"

"Say? What's to say? It's been two weeks; he doesn't call, he doesn't write . . ."

♦

Can you give me a couple of good Jewish wines?

I wanna go to Miami.
I wanna mink coat.
I wanna diamond ring.

♦

How do JAPs like to make love?

Facing Bloomingdale's.

♦

A JAP went to see her gynecologist for a checkup. After a complete examination, the doctor said, "That's the cleanest vagina I've ever seen."

"Why thank you, Doctor," the woman said. "I have a maid come in once a week."

♦

Harry and Abe had been friends almost all their lives. Now, as their time on earth drew to a close, Abe asked Harry, "Do you believe in life after death?" "I don't know," Harry said, "but we should make a pact: Whoever goes first will give the other a sign."

Not too long after, Abe died, and Harry waited for a sign. One day, the telephone rang. "Hello

Harry?" came the voice. "Abe!" Harry said. "Where are you?" "Well, where I am the grass is green, the air is sweet and pure, there are beautiful mountains. I get up in the morning, have a little grass, make a little love, take a little nap. In the afternoon, I have a little grass, make a little love, take a little nap. In the evening, I have a little grass, make a little love, and go to sleep." "You mean you're in heaven?" "Heaven? What heaven? I'm a buffalo in Montana."

♦

Did you hear about the alligators in Florida with little Jews on their T-shirts?

♦

How do you say "fuck you" in Yiddish?

Trust me.

♦

What's a JAP's idea of the perfect house?

Thirteen rooms; no kitchen and no bedroom.

♦

Two black men planned to smuggle a gorilla into the country. They racked their brains and finally came up with the idea of disguising the ape. They dressed the gorilla in tight Calvin Klein jeans and a silk shirt, put high heels on its feet and a blond wig on its head. They hung the beast with gold necklaces and bracelets and put a ring on every finger; sunglasses and a

Gucci bag were the finishing touches. They got the gorilla onto the plane without a problem, but as they approached JFK they began to sweat. At the customs gate, the two men were sure the jig was up when the agent stared long and hard at the gorilla. Then he said, "So nu? What's a nice Jewish girl like you doing with these two *schwartzes?*"

♦

What are three words a JAP has never heard?

Attention K-Mart shoppers.

♦

What was the first Israeli settlement?

Two cents on the dollar.

♦

Mr. Moskowitz went to the doctor for his yearly checkup, only to be told he had a terrible wasting disease and faced a long and lingering death. Horrified, he asked the doctor if there was any cure.

"There are no drugs that are effective, but there's a rather unorthodox treatment that's not officially condoned, but has been rather successful—mother's milk."

Mr. Moskowitz returned home distraught. On hearing the story, his wife said, "Sha! It's not that bad. Mrs. O'Hearn upstairs is nursing her eleventh. I'm certain if you explain the situation to her she'll be able to help."

Sure enough, when Mrs. O'Hearn heard Mr. Moskowitz's tale of woe, she immediately offered him her breast. As he suckled, Mrs. O'Hearn found herself getting quite excited.

"So Mr. Moskowitz," she said coyly, "is there anything else you'd like?"

Mr. Moskowitz looked up and said, "Maybe a cookie?"

♦

Why didn't the JAP want a colostomy?

Because she couldn't get shoes to match the bag.

♦

Mr. Greenstein went to the doctor.

"So what's your problem?" the doctor asked.

"I can't pee," Greenstein replied.

"Hmmm. How old are you?"

"Eighty-one."

"Don't you think you've peed enough?"

♦

How can you tell when a Jewish woman has an orgasm?

She drops her nail file.

♦

The first Martian expedition landed on Earth and was met by the press. A reporter looked at one of the Martians and said, "I see you have a pointed head. Does everyone on Mars have a pointed head?"

The Martian looked at him as though he were crazy, and said, "Of course."

"I see you have bright green hands and feet.

On Earth, this is very unusual. Does everyone on Mars have green hands and feet?"

The Martian replied, "Of course."

"You're wearing an enormous amount of gold jewelry," the reporter said. "Rings, bracelet, necklaces—I've never seen so much gold on one person before. Does everyone on Mars wear that much jewelry?"

"Not the *goyim.*"

♦

What's the difference between a JAP and Jell-O?

Jell-O moves when you eat it.

♦

Old Mr. Goldberg, after eating a seven-course meal in a downtown restaurant, announced to the waiter that he wasn't going to pay the bill because he'd found a hair in his rice pudding.

The waiter insisted that Mr. Goldberg pay the bill, but Mr. Goldberg ran out of the restaurant. The waiter, angered, ran after him. He didn't catch up to him until Mr. Goldberg had reached the neighborhood brothel.

The waiter explained to the madame that he must talk to Mr. Goldberg—could she please point out the room into which he had disappeared? The waiter slipped her a couple of bucks, and the madame pointed down the hall.

The waiter rushed into the indicated room to find Mr. Goldberg eating one of the girls. The waiter said, "For a hair in your rice pudding you won't pay your check, but you'll come to this place and eat her?!"

"That's right," answered the old Jew. "And if I

find rice pudding in her, I'm not paying her, either."

◆

Mrs. Goldblum brought her husband's remains to the undertaker to have cremated. When asked what kind of container she wanted his ashes stored in, she said, "None. I want them poured right into my hands."

The undertaker thought this rather odd, but did as the widow requested. Mrs. Goldblum returned home and went straight to the bedroom. She dimmed the lights, put romantic music on the stereo, and whispered, "Hymie, here's that blow job you always wanted!" And she blew his ashes all over the bed.

◆

How does a Jewish couple perform "doggie style" sex?

He sits up and begs and she lays down and plays dead.

Various Villainies

Why do female paratroopers wear jockstraps?

So they don't whistle on the way down.

♦

Susan was standing on a street corner when a man stopped and said, "Excuse me, miss, but did you know that you have a tampon hanging out of your mouth?" "Oh my God," she said. "What did I do with my cigarette?"

♦

Did you hear what happened to the fly on the toilet seat?

He got pissed off.

♦

Miss White asked her class to use the word "definitely" in a sentence.

Little Lucy raised her hand. "The sky is definitely blue."

"That was a very good answer, dear, but the sky is sometimes pink, or gray, too. 'Definitely' has a stronger meaning."

Jimmy raised his hand. "The grass is definitely green."

"Very good, Jimmy, but sometimes the grass is brown, or yellow."

Little Abie waved his hand. "Yes?" said the teacher.

"Teacher, does a fart have lumps?"

The teacher was horrified. "Abie, what are you talking about? Of course not!"

"Well then," said Abie, "I definitely have shit in my pants."

♦

Why are the starship *Enterprise* and toilet paper similar?

They both circle Uranus looking for Klingons.

♦

How can you tell a macho woman?

She rolls her own tampons.

♦

On the first day of kindergarten, the teacher instructed her class on the correct way to get her attention if they had to go to the bathroom.

"Now boys and girls, if you have to make a sissy you raise one finger, and if you have to move your bowels you raise two. Does everybody understand?"

Everybody nods their heads in unison.

All seems to be well. Then about a week later the teacher looks up to see a child frantically waving his hand.

"Why Johnny! What on earth is the matter!"

"Give me a number quick! I gotta fart!"

♦

Farmer Johnson was drunk again.

"You know, Anna," he said to his long-suffering wife, "if you could only lay eggs we could get rid of all those smelly chickens."

Anna said nothing. Farmer Johnson tried again.

"You know, Anna, if only you could give milk we could get rid of that expensive herd of cows."

Anna looked at him coolly. "You know, Jack," she said, "if only you could get it up we could get rid of your brother Bob."

♦

What do you call a child raised in a house of ill repute?

A brothel sprout.

♦

What do the Rockettes and the circus have in common?

The circus is a cunning array of stunts.

♦

How would you describe a cow after an abortion?

De-calf-inated.

♦

A drunk walks into a bar and says to the bartender, "If I can make my ass sing, do I get a free drink?" The bartender says sure. The drunk jumps up on the bar and takes a disgusting dump. The patrons go screaming out into the streets. The bartender is furious. "Why the hell did you do that?!!" he screams. The drunk responds, "Hey, even Perry Como has to clear his throat."

◆

How can you tell if a woman is wearing pantyhose?

Her ankles swell when she farts.

◆

A contest was being held at the circus: A hundred-dollar prize was being offered to the first person who could make the elephant nod his head up and down.

Dozens of people tried and failed. Finally, a little old man walked over to the elephant and grabbed its balls; the elephant roared in pain and tossed its head up and down. The old man collected his prize money and departed.

The next year a similar contest was held using the same elephant; the difference was that the winner had to make the animal shake its head from side to side. Again dozens tried and failed. Finally, the same little old man who walked off with the money the previous year appeared. He walked up to the elephant.

"Remember me?" he said.

The elephant shook its head up and down.

"Want me to do what I did to you last year?"

The elephant shook its head back and forth violently.

The man walked off with the prize money.

♦

What do you get when a canary flies into a screen door?

Shredded tweet.

♦

Tom met his friend Brent on the street.

"How are you doing?" asked Tom.

"Not good," answered Brent. "I've had a sore throat for weeks."

"Really?" asked Tom. "I had that same problem awhile back."

"No kidding," said Brent. "How'd you get rid of it?"

"Well," replied Tom, "don't laugh, but my wife gave me a blow job, and it went away like that."

"That's great!" responded Brent. "Do you think she's home now?"

♦

How do you get a tissue to dance?

Blow a little boogie into it.

♦

What happens when you cross an elephant and a prostitute?

You get a hooker who does it for peanuts and doesn't forget you.

♦

Michael was a handsome young man with a terrible problem: severe flatulence. On his first date with a stunning young woman, he was able to control himself for most of the evening, but finally, he needed desperately to get home. Unfortunately, his date insisted that he come home with her to meet her parents.

Sitting in the living room with the family dog, Baron, at his side, Michael could no longer fight nature. He let out an audible fart.

"Baron!" yelled the father.

Thank God, thought Michael.

Not too many minutes passed before Michael had to relieve himself again.

"Baron!" yelled the father again.

Michael relaxed. But nature would not be denied, and this time he really let one roar.

"Baron!" screamed the father. "Get away from that man before he shits all over you!"

♦

Why did they kick the midget out of the nudist colony?

He was getting into everybody's hair.

♦

What do a coffin and a condom have in common?

They're both filled with stiffs—only one's coming and one's going.

♦

What's brown and sits on a piano bench?

Beethoven's first movement.

♦

What's brown and has holes in it?

Swiss shit.

♦

Why did the man with the legless dog call his pet "Cigarette?"

Because every so often he'd take him for a drag.

♦

A very attractive, well-dressed man was having a great night picking up women at a midtown bar. A drunk at the other end of the bar, viewing the man's success, was impressed. After the man returned from his third conquest of the evening, the drunk sat next to him and asked him for his secret for picking up women.

"It's easy," said the man. "I just smile and say 'Tickle your ass with a feather?' If she likes the idea, I'm in. If she says 'Excuse me?', I say 'It's starting to trickle outside; awfully nasty weather,' then move on to someone else."

"Got ya," says the drunk.

Half an hour later, the man had left and the drunk had finished another half quart of Scotch. Having spotted his quarry, the drunk staggered up to the woman and said loudly, "Stick a feather up your ass?"

Shocked, she replied, "Excuse me?"
"I said," said the drunk, "it's raining like a fuck outside."

♦

Have you heard that there's a new line of designer jeans called Crisco?

It's for the woman with fat in the can.

♦

How do you know that a female bartender is pissed off at you?

There's a string hanging out of your Bloody Mary.

♦

Mr. Hudson came home to find his wife sitting naked in front of the mirror, admiring her breasts.
"What do you think you're doing?" he asked.
"I went to the doctor today and he said I have the breasts of a twenty-five-year-old."
"Oh, yeah? And what did he have to say about your fifty-year-old ass?"
"Nothing," she replied. "Your name didn't come up at all."

♦

When it was time for milk and cookies at the nursery school, Joey refused to line up with the rest of the class.
"What's the matter, Joey?" asked the teacher. "Don't you want any cookies today?"

"Fuck you and your milk and cookies," Joey answered.

Shocked, the teacher figured the best way to handle the incident was to ignore it. But the next day when it came time for milk and cookies she got the same reply: "Fuck you and your milk and cookies."

This time the teacher called Joey's mother. She came to class the next day and when milk and cookies time arrived, she hid in the closet.

The teacher asked Joey if he wanted his snack and he replied: "Fuck you and your milk and cookies."

She opened the closet door and asked Joey's mother what she thought of her son's vulgar language.

"Well, fuck him, don't give him any!"

♦

What's the difference between a pigmy tribe and an all-girl track team?

Pigmies are cunning runts.

♦

What's green and skates?

Peggy Phlegm.

♦

What's green and slides down the hospital walls?

Mucus Welby.

◆

Four nuns were outside the confessional, waiting their turn to ask forgiveness for their sins. The first nun went in and said, "Forgive me Father, for I have sinned. I have put my finger on a man's penis."

The priest said, "Say five Our Fathers and put your finger in holy water."

The second nun went in and said, "Forgive me Father, for I have sinned. I have put my hand on a man's penis."

The priest said, "Say five Our Fathers and put your hand in holy water."

When she heard this, the third nun turned to the fourth and said, "Maybe you should go in first, Sister, since I'll have to douche after you gargle."

◆

What's grosser than gross?

When you kiss your grandmother and she slips you the tongue.

◆

Why do you wrap a hamster in electrician's tape?

So it won't explode when you fuck it.

During the science lesson the teacher asked her third graders if they could tell her how a cat's tail was connected to its body.

"How about you, Jimmy?" said the teacher. "Come up here and use the model on my desk."

Little Jimmy approached the model and studied it thoroughly.

"Well, by the look of those nuts I'd say the damn thing's bolted on!"

What's green and flies over Berlin?

Snotzies.

What is this?

0
B.A.
M.A.
PhD.

Three degrees below zero.

What is this a picture of?

Two men walking abreast.

♦

A man gets drunk at a party, and his friends call a cab to take him home. Once in the cab, the man starts to tell the cabby about his life: how lonely he's been since his wife left him, how hard his job is, how no one appreciates him. "You seem like a nice guy," the drunk says.

"Yeah," says the cabby indifferently.

"What do you say? Do you think there's room in the front seat for a pizza and a couple of six-packs?"

The driver thinks about it for a minute and says, "Sure, why not?"

"Gee, thanks," says the drunk, leans over the partition and throws up.

♦

How do you find a foxhole?

Lift its tail.

♦

What's so great about being a test-tube baby?

You have a womb with a view.

♦

A man walks into a bar and asks the bartender for a shot of forty-year-old Scotch. Not wanting to go down to the basement and deplete his supply of the rare and expensive liquor, the bartender pours a shot of ten-year-old Scotch and figures that his customer won't be able to tell the difference.

The man downs the Scotch and says, "My good man, that Scotch is only ten years old. I specifically asked for forty-year-old Scotch."

Amazed, the bartender reaches into a locked cabinet underneath the bar and pulls out a bottle of twenty-year-old Scotch and pours the man a shot. The customer drinks it down and says, "That was twenty-year-old Scotch. I asked for forty-year-old Scotch."

So the bartender goes into the back room and brings out a bottle of thirty-year-old Scotch and pours the customer a drink. By now a small crowd has gathered around the man and is watching anxiously as he downs the latest drink. Once again the man states the true age of the Scotch and repeats his original request.

The bartender can hold off no longer and disappears into the cellar to get a bottle of prime forty-year-old Scotch. As the bartender returns with the drink, an old drunk who had been watching the proceedings with interest leaves the bar and returns with a full shot glass of his own.

The customer downs the Scotch and says, "Now this is forty-year-old Scotch!" The crowd applauds his discriminating palate.

"I bet you think you're real smart," slurs the drunk. "Here, take a swig of this."

Rising to the challange, the man takes the glass and downs the drink in one swallow. Immediately, he chokes and spits out the liquid on the barroom floor.

"My God!" he exclaims. "That's piss!"

"Great guess," says the drunk. "Now tell me how old I am."

◆

What's the difference between a fox and a pig?

Six drinks.

◆

What's red and white and lives in a test tube?

Bozo the Clone.

◆

What do you call a limbless man in a pool?

Bob.

◆

What do you call a limbless man on a wall?

Art.

◆

What do you call a limbless man in a pile of leaves?

Russell.

◆

What do you call a limbless man on a doorstep?

Matt.

◆

What's a real friend?

Someone who will go downtown, get two blow jobs, come back and give you one.

◆

With his thirtieth wedding anniversary only a week away, Mr. Fairweather stopped in at the best furrier in town.

"I'd like to speak to Al," said Mr. Fairweather, who knew that Al owned the posh store.

"I'm Al," said the man standing near a rack of dark furs. "What can I do for you?"

"Well," said Mr. Fairweather, "next week's my thirtieth anniversary, and I want to buy my wife the best fur in town."

Mr. Fairweather did not look all that wealthy, so Al said, "How about a lovely raccoon coat?"

"No," replied Mr. Fairweather. "My wife got one of those on our tenth anniversary."

"Well, how about a nice ranch mink?"

"Sorry," said Mr. Fairweather. "She got that on our twentieth. Do you have something more interesting—more out of the ordinary?"

"Well," suggested Al, "we do have something a bit unusual. How would your wife like a full-length skunk coat?"

"Skunk! Isn't that a rodent?"

"Nah," replied Al. "It's just a pussy that smells bad."

"Thanks anyway," said Mr. Fairweather. "She's got one of those too!"

◆

Why do women have legs?

So they don't leave snail tracks on linoleum floors.

♦

Why do women have two holes so close together?

In case you miss.

♦

A man goes into a restaurant and orders soup. When the waiter brings out the bowl he has his thumb stuck in the soup, but the customer decides to let this pass.

"Would you like anything else?" the waiter inquires. "We have some very good beef stew today."

"Sounds good," says the customer. So the waiter goes off and comes back with a plate of stew, and his thumb is in the stew. The customer is getting angry, but decides to hold his tongue.

"How about some hot apple pie?" asks the waiter.

"Fine," says the customer. The waiter returns, with his thumb stuck in the pie. Now the customer is really getting furious.

"Coffee?" asks the waiter, and when the customer nods yes, he hurries off. He returns with his thumb stuck in the cup of coffee. By now the customer can no longer restrain himself.

"What the hell do you think you're doing? Everytime you've come to the table you've had your thumb stuck in my food!"

"I've got an infection and my doctor told me to keep my thumb in a hot moist place."

"Why don't you just stick it up your ass?"

"Where do you think I put it when I'm in the kitchen?"

◆

Mr. Jones went to apply for Social Security. He stepped up to the counter, where the clerk asked for his identification and proof of age. After he presented her with the documents, the clerk requested that he pull up his shirt and show her his chest. Mr. Jones complied, and the clerk gave him his first month's check. Bewildered, Mr. Jones returned home and told his wife what had happened. "Too bad you didn't drop your pants for her," she said. "You could have gotten disability too."

◆

What species of deer is found near pickle factories?

Dill does.

◆

John walks into the bar to look for his friend Bob. After finding him, he proceeds to tell him how much he hates his wife.

"Why don't you have her murdered?" asks Bob. "I know a guy, Artie, who'll do it for you cheap."

This sounds good to John, so Bob sets up a meeting. Artie and John come to an understanding; they agree on a date, a time, and the fee of a dollar.

Artie goes to John's apartment as planned and strangles John's wife. Unfortunately, the maid walks in before he can escape; Artie strangles her so there will be no witnesses. On his way down the stairs he encounters John's mother-in-law; she, too, has got to go.

Unfortunately for Artie, someone tipped off the police, and he is captured as he walks out the front door.

The next day's headlines read: ARTIE CHOKES THREE FOR A DOLLAR.

♦

A woman shopping in the supermarket keeps fondling herself as she walks up and down the aisles. Several of the customers complain to the manager, who confronts the woman.

"Madam," he says, "if you continue to touch yourself in that manner I'll have to ask you to leave the store."

"But this is how I remember what I'm supposed to buy," she replies. "When I do this," she says, holding her head in her hands, "I remember to buy a head of lettuce. When I do this," she says as she grabs her breasts, "I remember to buy chicken breasts. And when I do this," she says, rubbing her crotch, "I know I won't forget to buy Fantastik!"

How do you recycle a used tampon?

As a tea bag for vampires.

What's the difference between a woman kneeling in prayer and a woman kneeling in the bathtub?

The woman kneeling in prayer has hope in her soul.

Eye-talians, or Never Let a Dago By

What's the difference between an elephant and an Italian grandmother?

Twenty pounds and a black dress.

♦

What does eating pussy and being a member of the Mafia have in common?

One slip of the tongue and you're in deep shit.

♦

Maria is sitting on her stoop eating a slice of pizza. Two of her girl friends walk by, and notice that she's not wearing any underwear.

"Hey, Maria," one of them calls, "did you take off your panties to keep yourself cool?"

"I don't know about keeping cool," Maria replies, "but it sure keeps the flies away from my pizza!"

♦

Did you hear about the Italian girl who thought a sanitary belt was a drink from a clean shot glass?

♦

How do you kill an Italian?

Smash the toilet seat over his head while he's getting a drink of water.

◆

Why don't Italians eat fleas?

Because they can't get their little legs apart.

◆

Two Italian carpenters are building a house. The foreman tells his assistant to get him some nails. After waiting for quite awhile for the assistant to return, the foreman goes off to see what's keeping the man. He finds him picking up one nail and putting it to one side, picking up another and putting it in another pile. Peeved, the foreman asks, "And what do you think you're doing?"

"Well," the assistant replies, "you're hammering into the right-hand wall, and all these nails point left."

"You idiot!" the foreman yells. "Those are for the other side of the house!"

◆

Why is Italy shaped like a boot?

Do you think they could fit all that shit in a tennis shoe?

◆

Why does the new Italian navy use glass-bottomed boats?

So they can steer clear of the old Italian navy.

◆

How can you tell an Italian plane out on the runway?

It's the one with hair under its wings.

♦

Three doctors were sitting around drinking coffee one morning after doing early operations.

"Boy," said the first doctor. "The operation I performed this morning was the easiest ever."

"Bet mine was easier," said the second doctor.

"I'm *sure* mine was the easiest," said the third.

"I don't know about that," said the first doctor. "I operated on a German guy today."

"I operated on a Chinaman."

"I operated on an Italian."

"Germans have got to be the easiest," said the first doctor. "You open them up and they have wheels and gears inside. You simply change a wheel or gear and close."

The second doctor said, "You're wrong. The Chinese are the easiest to operate on. They have color-coded transistors; just change a defective transistor, and you're done."

"You're both wrong—Italians are by far the easiest to operate on. They only have two moving parts—the mouth and the asshole—and they're interchangeable!"

♦

How can you tell a rich Italian?

He's the one with whitewalls on his cement mixer.

♦

Did you hear about the flamingos in Florida with little pink cement Italians on their lawns?

♦

Why did Mrs. Minellis have thirteen children?

She thought you had to be black to use the rhythm method.

♦

What do you call a mole on an Italian's ass?

A brain tumor.

♦

An Italian couple are spending their wedding night at the house of the bride's parents. Rosa sits on the bed as her husband undresses. He takes off his shirt and she sees the thick hair covering his chest. Terribly upset, she runs downstairs to her mother.

"Mama," she screams. "He's got hair all over his chest like an animal!"

"Calm down," her mother says, "and go back upstairs. It's your wifely duty."

Up she goes, just in time to see her husband remove his trousers. Again the bride bolts from the room and runs to her mother.

"Mama, he's got hair all over his legs like a monkey!"

"Silly girl, go back upstairs and make love to your husband like a good Italian wife."

Once again she returns to the bedroom to find

her husband removing his shoes, and he has only half of a foot on his left leg.

She runs downstairs and gasps, "Mama, he has a foot and a half!"

Her mother pushes her aside. "Stupid girl! You stay down here and *I'll* go upstairs!"

◆

Why did the Italian trade in his wife for a garbage can?

Because it had a smaller hole and it smelled better.

◆

Define "cad."

An Italian who doesn't tell his wife he's sterile until after she's pregnant.

◆

Mr. Mastrianni had a terrible problem—he hadn't had a bowel movement in two weeks. When he explained the situation to his doctor, the doctor gave him a box of suppositories and told him to use them all and come back in a week.

Unfortunately, Mr. Mastrianni had never used suppositories before; he supposed they were simply very large pills. So he ate two the first day, four the next, and so on until the box was finished and the week was up.

He returned to the doctor and said, "Doctor, I did what you told me and I still have no relief."

The doctor was amazed. "I don't understand! You've used a whole box of these and you still haven't gone? What have you been doing, eating them?"

"What do you think I've been doing? Shoving them up my ass?"

In a Word, Sex

Did you hear about the little boy who, while passing his parent's bedroom, stared in and said, "And you have the nerve to slap me for sucking my thumb!"

♦

An old whore walks into a bar with a parrot on her finger.

"I'll fuck the first guy here who can guess this parrot's weight!"

After a long silence a drunk in the back yells out, "Five hundred pounds!"

"Close enough!"

♦

What do Rubik's Cube and a penis have in common?

The longer you play with it, the harder it gets.

♦

What's a 68?

You do me and I owe you one.

♦

Sally arrived home from her date on a cloud. She tossed her coat over a chair, her purse over the banister; she threw the rest of her clothing around her bedroom with abandon.

The next morning at breakfast her mother asked if she had a good time.

"Oh," sighed Sally, "I had a *wonderful* time!"

"I guess so," her mother remarked. "Your underpants are still stuck to the ceiling."

♦

What's the modern woman's idea of the perfect man?

One who's two-and-a-half feet tall, has a ten-inch tongue, and can breathe through his ears.

♦

A boy baby and a girl baby are lying together in their crib. All of a sudden, the girl baby starts to scream, "Rape! Rape! Somebody help me! Rape! Rape!"

Her companion looks at her and says, "Oh, shut up! You just rolled over on my pacifier."

♦

What's the difference between men and jelly beans?

Jelly beans come in different colors.

♦

A man spending the afternoon with his married lover hears her husband return unexpectedly. He hops out of bed, grabs his clothes, and ducks into the closet. Behind him he hears a whisper, "Boy, it sure is dark in here!"

"Who's that?"

"My name's Johnny, and I live here. Do you

wanna buy my marble collection? Only a hundred bucks."

"A hundred bucks? Are you crazy?" asks the man.

"Well, if you're not interested maybe my father—"

"No, wait! Here's the hundred, now shut up!"

Two days later, in the same bed, the man hears his lover's husband return. Again he takes cover in the closet, and hears a small voice behind him say, "Boy, it sure is dark in here!"

"You again?"

"Yeah, and this time I'm selling my baseball card collection."

"Okay, how much this time?"

"Two hundred. Inflation, you know."

"Jesus! Here. Now shut up!"

The next day the boy boasts about his windfall to his father, who says, "I don't know what you did to get that much money, but it couldn't have been honest. You'd better go to confession."

So the boy goes to church and takes his place in the confessional. He says in a whisper, "Boy, it sure is dark in here!"

At that the priest's partition opens with a bang, and the priest says, "Are you going to start that shit again?"

◆

What do a virgin and a sneeze have in common?

Goes in tight.

◆

Why isn't being a penis all it's cracked up to be?

You have a head but no brains, there are always a couple of nuts following you around all the time, your next door neighbor is an asshole, and your best friend is a cunt.

◆

A horny pair of teenagers are driving down the highway; they can't keep their hands off one another. The young man, very aroused, says to his girl friend, "Let's pull over and do it by the side of the road."

"But people driving by will be able to see into the car," she protests.

The boy pulls over on an incline off the highway. "Look, we'll get underneath the car, and I'll leave my feet sticking out. If anyone comes by I'll tell them I'm fixing the muffler."

Reluctantly, the girl agrees, so they wriggle underneath the car and start to make love. All of a sudden, the young man feels someone kicking his foot.

"And just what do you think you're doing?" a policeman asks.

"Fixing my muffler," the boy replies.

"Well, you should have fixed your brakes first; your car just rolled down the hill."

◆

How many mice does it take to screw in a light bulb?

Two, but don't ask me how they got there.

◆

What's the difference between kinky and perverted?

Kinky is when you tickle your lover's ass with a feather. Perverted is when you use the whole chicken.

♦

Mrs. Schwartz decided she should learn to play golf. She signed up for lessons with the pro at the country club, but after six months she could still barely get the ball off the tee. At the end of his patience, the pro finally said, "Mrs. Schwartz, there's only one thing left that I can think of to try with you. No matter how strange my instructions sound, just do what I say. I want you to hold the club as though it were your husband's penis, and hit the ball." This was indeed strange, but Mrs. Schwartz was willing to try anything. She followed the pro's instructions, and lo and behold, the ball went 300 yards straight down the fairway. "Wonderful!" said the pro. "Now take the club out of your mouth—"

♦

Why does an elephant have four feet?

Because eight inches isn't enough.

♦

What do soybeans and dildos have in common?

They're both meat substitutes.

♦

What has a thousand teeth and holds back a monster?

My zipper.

♦

What do a virgin and a hemophiliac have in common?

One prick and it's all over.

♦

How does a woman hold her liquor?

By the ears.

♦

Did you hear about the merger of Xerox and Wurlitzer?

The new company will make reproductive organs.

♦

The young brave went to his chief and said, "Me want squaw."

"Do you have experience?" the chief asked.

"No," the boy replied. "How me get experience?"

"Go into the woods, find tree with knothole, and practice. Come back in two weeks and I will give you squaw."

The boy left and, as instructed, returned in two weeks.

"You have experience?" asked the chief. The boy nodded. "Good, now you have experience you can have squaw. Little Flower, come here! This brave has no experience with woman. You treat him well and guide him."

Smiling, Little Flower took the young brave by the hand and led him to her teepee. There, after they had undressed, the brave told Little Flower to turn around and bend over. Puzzled, she complied, then shrieked when he kicked her in the ass.

"What you do that for?" she asked.

"Me no stupid. Me check for bees!"

◆

A little boy walked in on his mom while she was taking a bath.

"What's that?" he asked, pointing to her pubic hair.

"It's my face cloth, sweetheart," she answers.

"Oh yeah," he says. "I saw the maid washing Daddy's face with one last night."

◆

What's the square root of 69?

Ate something.

◆

What's better than four roses on a piano?

Two lips on an organ.

◆

What do butter and a hooker have in common?

They both spread for bread.

A traveling saleswoman was driving through a remote rural area in the south when her car broke down. She took to the road and eventually came to a small farmhouse. On the front porch sat two men in rocking chairs.

"How far is it to the nearest gas station?" she asked.

"Oh, about twenty miles, I reckon," drawled one man.

"Well, how far is it to the nearest hotel?"

"I guess that would be about thirty miles," answered his companion.

"Could you drive me there?"

"Don't have no car."

Despairing, the woman said, "Do you think I could possibly stay with you tonight? I'm sure I'll be able to hitch a ride in the morning."

"Sure you can. But you'll have to share our bed."

The woman had no other choice but to agree. Before she got into bed that night, she handed each man a rubber and said, "Please wear these so I won't get pregnant."

The next morning she left. Three months later, the two men are sitting on the porch when one says to the other, "Say Bob, do you care if that there saleslady gets pregnant?"

"Nope."

"Then what do you say we take these damn things off."

What's the difference between "ohh" and "ahh"?

About four inches.

♦

A farmer was having trouble getting his chicken to lay eggs, so he brought in a rooster who had a reputation as (you should pardon the expression) a legendary cocksman. The rooster got right to work, and soon there were eggs all over the place. His job done, the rooster went after the pigs, the ducks, the sheep, and would have gone after a snake if someone had held its head. The farmer, afraid of losing the bird, tried to get him to calm down, but with no luck. One morning he found the rooster flat on his back, eyes closed—apparently dead of exhaustion. When he started to berate the corpse, the rooster opened one eye and said "Shh! You see those buzzards up there?"

♦

Define "virgin."

An ugly third grader.

♦

What's organic dental floss?

Pubic hair.

♦

When does a Cub Scout become a Boy Scout?

When he eats his first Brownie.

♦

Moskowitz, Horowitz, and Shapiro went on safari, where they were set upon by a large tribe of fierce and hostile savages. Bound and helpless, they were brought before the chief. Pointing to Moskowitz, he says, "You have a choice. Death or bunda."

Moskowitz says "What could be worse than death? Bunda!"

He's seized and viciously sodomized by the entire tribe.

The next day the chief says to Horowitz, "Death or bunda?"

Horowitz, shaking, says, "Bunda." He too is abused by the whole tribe.

The next day the chief stands in front of Shapiro and says, "Death or bunda?" Shapiro looks him straight in the eye and says, "Death."

"Terrific!" says the chief. "Death by bunda!"

♦

What do women and spaghetti have in common?

They both squirm when you eat them.

♦

What's a 72?

69 with three people watching.

What do you call a female clone?

A clunt.

Where is an elephant's sex organ?

In his feet: If he steps on you, you're fucked.

What did the hurricane say to the coconut tree?

Hold on to your nuts; this ain't gonna be no ordinary blow job.

What do you call a happy Roman?

Glad he ate her.

On their first date, Joe took Rose to the carnival. When he asked her what she wanted to do first, Rose replied, "Get weighed."

So Joe took her to the man with the scale who guesses your weight. He looked at Rose and said, "One hundred and twenty pounds." Since Rose weighed in at one seventeen, she collected a prize.

Next they went on the roller coaster. When the ride was finished, Joe asked Rose what she wanted to do next. "Get weighed," she said. So they went back to the man with the scale, who of course guessed Rose's weight correctly. Leaving without a prize, they went for a ride on the merry-go-round. After they got off, Joe asked Rose what she wanted to do. "I want to get weighed!" she said again.

Now Joe began to think this girl was quite strange, and decided to end the evening quickly. He left her at the door with a quick handshake.

Rose's roommate was waiting up for her to return and asked how the evening went.

"Wousy!"

♦

Did you hear about the new designer condom?

Sergio Preventes.

♦

Is sex better than pot?

It depends on the pusher.

♦

Saul, who was three feet, five inches tall, was asked how he had liked his stay at the nudist colony.

"It was kind of scary," he replied. "Everyone looked like Fidel Castro."

♦

One sunny day a bunny rabbit was walking along the water's edge when he saw an island.

Straining his eyes, the bunny spied what looked like hundreds of thousands of carrot leaves. "Boy," thought the bunny, "if I could just get over to that island, I'd be the happiest bunny in the world."

Now bunnies hate water, but all those delicious carrots proved a huge temptation to our bunny, and he decided to try to get out to the island. Getting up all his courage, he took three running hops and PLOP! landed right in the middle of the island. What he'd seen from shore were indeed carrot leaves, and he began to munch happily away on all the carrots a rabbit could want. "I *am* the happiest bunny in the world," thought the rabbit as he hopped happily along eating carrots.

About half an hour later, a cat was walking along the shore and saw the rabbit hopping happily away on the island. Her eyes not being as good (for she didn't eat carrots), she had no idea that it was all those carrots that were making the bunny so happy. "Boy," she thought, "look how happy that bunny is. If I could just get over to that island, I'd be the happiest cat in the world."

Cats hate water even more than bunnies do, but our cat was determined to be as happy as that bunny was. Getting up all her courage, she crouched, sprang, and SPLASH! landed in the water and drowned.

The moral of the story: Behind every satisfied Peter is a wet pussy.

◆

A little boy walks in on his mother while she's taking a bath.

"What's that?" he asks, pointing at his mother's pubic hair.

"That's where Daddy hit me with an axe," she answers.

Wide-eyed the boy says, "You mean right in the cunt?!"

♦

What do you call a truck full of vibrators?

Toys for twats.

♦

Preparing to walk through the dangerous woods to see her grandmother, Little Red Riding Hood puts her father's gun in her picnic basket.

On the way, she is stopped by the Big Bad Wolf.

"Little Red Riding Hood, I'm going to rape you," growls the wolf.

Drawing her gun Little Red Riding Hood declares, "Oh, no, you're not. You're going to eat me, just like the story says."

♦

A man walked into a bar with a dog at his side. "Get that dog out of here," ordered the bartender.

The dog's owner became indignant. "This here dog isn't just any old dog," he said. "He's the smartest dog in the whole world."

"Oh yeah? Prove it!" challenged the bartender.

Turning to the dog, the man said, "Rex, here's a buck. Go get me a pack of Luckies."

The dog ran out the door and, within a few minutes, returned with the cigarettes and some matches in a little brown bag.

The bartender was impressed. "Maybe that dog *is* really smart. How about if I give him fifteen dollars and ask him to bring me back a bag of pot from the local dealer?"

"Sure," said the dog's owner. The bartender gave the dog money and directions, and the dog was on his way.

Ten minutes went by.

Half an hour.

After an hour, the dog still hadn't returned.

By this time, the bartender, sure he'd been cheated, threw the dog's owner out of the bar.

The man wandered several blocks in search of his errant mutt. Finally he came to an alley, and there was Rex screwing a mangy-looking French poodle.

"Why, you son of a bitch," screamed the man, separating the two dogs. "You really blew the act this time. How could you do this to me? You've never done anything like this before!"

"True," replied the dog. "But I never had fifteen dollars before, either."

♦

Little Red Riding Hood was walking through the woods when the Big Bad Wolf jumped out of the bushes and said, "Now I've got you and I'm going to eat you!"

"Eat, eat, eat," said Little Red Riding Hood. "Doesn't anybody just fuck anymore?"

♦

A really conceited man is screwing a really conceited woman.
"Aren't I tight?" she asks.
"No," he replies, "just full."

♦

What's 69 and 69?

Dinner for four.

♦

What's the difference between your sister and a Cadillac?

Most people haven't been in a Cadillac.

♦

And then there was the man who bought his wife a glass diaphragm because he wanted a womb with a view.

♦

What's the difference between a prostitute and a rooster?

A rooster says "Cock-a-doodle-doo."

A prostitute says "Any cock will do."

♦

Two fleas met on the beach in Miami; one of them had a terrible cold.

"What happened to you?" asked his friend.

"I came down on the moustache of a man on a motorcycle."

"Look, next year, you go to the airport, get on a toilet seat in the stewardesses' lounge, and you'll have a nice soft warm ride down."

"Sounds good," wheezed the flea. "I'll try it."

The next winter the two fleas met on the beach again; the same flea had a terrible cold again.

"What happened?" asked his friend. "Didn't you take my advice?"

"Sure I did. I went to the airport, parked myself on a toilet seat in the stewardesses' lounge, and when one sat down, I hopped aboard. It was so soft and warm and comfy that I fell asleep—and woke up on the moustache of a man on a motorcycle."

♦

Why don't chickens need underwear?

Because their peckers are on their faces.

♦

What's worse than getting raped by Jack the Ripper?

Being fingered by Captain Hook.

♦

What do you call a midget's circumcision?

Tiny trim.

♦

What's yellow and lays in a tree?

Tweety the whore.

♦

Did you hear about the guy who got herpes on his eyelids?

He was looking for love in all the wrong places.

♦

A guy was screwing his girl friend in the backseat of his car when a cop comes by and says, "What do you think you're doing?"

The man rolls down his window and answers, "I'm screwing my girl."

"Good!" says the cop. "I'm next."

"Sounds good to me," says the guy. "I've never screwed a cop before."

♦

What do you get when you cross a rooster with a telephone pole?

A twelve-foot cock that wants to reach out and touch someone.

♦

A lumberjack went to a brothel and asked for the meanest, toughest girl in the house.

"I know just the girl for you," said the madame. "Go ahead upstairs—second room on the left—and I'll send her up." He started up the stairs.

"Oh," yelled the madame after him. "Is there anything else you'd like?"

"Yeah," he replied from the top of the stairs, "a six-pack would be nice."

The lumberjack entered the room and sat down. A few minutes later, in came a big bruiser of a woman, naked and carrying a six-pack.

The lumberjack liked what he saw, and couldn't wait to get started. The big woman was just what he was looking for. But before he could make a move for her, she got down on all fours, arched her back, and thrust her ass at him.

Incredibly excited, the lumberjack asked, "Wow, what's that position called?

"Position? What position?" the big whore replied. "I thought you'd want to open the beer first."

♦

What do you get when you cross a donkey with an onion?

A piece off ass that brings tears to your eyes.

♦

What do a spider's web and a passionate kiss have in common?

They both end in the undoing of a fly.

◆

What do you call a woman who can suck an orange through a garden hose?

Darling.

Poles and the Pope

What did the Polish woman say to her unmarried pregnant daughter?

Don't worry, maybe it's not yours.

♦

Why do Poles carry turds in their wallets?

For identification.

♦

Have you heard about the Polish parachute?

It opens on impact.

♦

Why is a Polish woman like a hockey team?

They both take showers after three periods.

♦

Do you know what happened when the last pope died?

Another one just poped up.

♦

Why do Poles smear shit on the walls at Polish weddings?

To keep the flies off the bride.

♦

Did you hear about the Pole whose dog got pregnant?

He was so upset that he married her.

♦

How can you tell when a Polish woman is having her period?

She's only wearing one sock.

And what do most Polish women die from?

Toxic Sock Syndrome.

♦

Did you hear about the Pole who thought manual labor was a famous Spanish painter?

♦

Sign in a Polish men's room—

"Please Don't Eat the Toilet Mint"

♦

Did you hear about the Polish chorus girl who thought Fucking was the capital of China?

♦

Two Poles were walking down the street when they saw a dog licking his balls.

"Gee," said the first man, "I wish I could do that."

His friend responded, "Don't you think you ought to pet him first?"

♦

Why is Pope John trying to recruit more blacks into the priesthood?

So they can teach the rhythm method to the masses.

♦

What do you call a Pole in a tree?

A branch manager.

♦

The Pole walked into the store, went up to the counter, and ordered a pound of *kielbassa* and a dozen *pirogen*. The counterman asked, "You're Polish, aren't you?"

"Why, yes," the man replied. "I'll bet you knew from my taste in food."

"No," said the counter man. "This is a drugstore."

♦

Did you hear about the Pole who thought Moby Dick was a venereal disease?

♦

Why don't they have ice cubes in Poland?

They lost the recipe.

♦

Why do Polish men make such lousy lovers?

Because they always wait for the swelling to go down.

♦

How can you tell the pope's private plane in a snowstorm?

It's the one with the chains on the propellers.

♦

Did you hear what happened to the Polish dog?

The tree pissed on him.

♦

Did you hear about the Polish gardener who broke his arm while he was raking leaves?

He fell out of the tree.

♦

Where do they hide the money in a Polish household?

Under the soap.

♦

Why did the Polish elevator operator lose his job?

He kept forgetting the route.

♦

Why did the Pole go through the car wash a second time?

He liked the special effects but he couldn't understand the ending.

♦

Why didn't the pope attend his own investiture?

He couldn't find a clean bowling shirt.

♦

Why did the city paint its manhole covers orange?

So the Poles would think they were eating at Howard Johnson's.

♦

Did you hear about the Polish college student?

He stayed up all night to study for a urine test—and failed.

♦

How do you get three Poles off a couch?

Jerk one off and the other two come.

♦

What do you call this? (Puff out your cheeks.)

A Polish sperm bank.

♦

Why aren't there any Polish cheerleaders?

Because they stick to the floor when they do splits.

♦

Did you hear about the Pole who bought a pair of Odor Eaters, took two steps and disappeared?

♦

Did you hear about the Polish newlyweds who didn't know the difference between K-Y jelly and putty?

Their windows fell out.

Fruits and Nuts

Define "organ grinder."

A gay with a chipped front tooth.

♦

Did you hear about the gay Polish bank robber?

He tied up the safe and blew the tellers.

♦

How can you separate the men from the boys in a gay bar?

With a crowbar.

♦

What do senators use instead of bookmarks?

Bent-over pages.

♦

Two gay lovers were having a quarrel.
"Go to hell!" screamed one.
"Drop dead!" screamed the other.
"Kiss my ass!"
"Oh, you *do* want to make up!"

♦

What do you call two homosexuals named Bob?

Oral Roberts.

♦

Define "frenzy."

Five hundred blind lesbians locked in a tuna factory.

♦

What do you call a gay with a vasectomy?

A seedless fruit.

♦

Did you hear about the two Scottish gays?

Ben Dover and Phil MacCrevice.

♦

A trucker driving through a small town stopped at a local bar and grill, looking forward to some supper and maybe a little excitement.

After ordering the blue-plate special, the trucker called the waiter over again and asked, "Hey, buddy, can ya tell me where a guy might find a little pussy around here? I've been on the road for two weeks and haven't had any in a long while—I'm really horny."

"Sorry, man," replied the waiter. "No women around here."

Discouraged, the trucker finished his meal and went to the game room to play a game of pool. Half an hour later, he summoned the waiter again.

"Hey, buddy, are you sure there ain't no women around here? I'm really in need of a good lay."

"Well," said the waiter, "if you're really desperate, you can fuck old Wong the Chinaman." He pointed to an old Chinese man sweeping the floor in the backroom.

"Hey, man," said the trucker, "I don't go for that shit. I want some pussy."

"Up to you," replied the waiter, wandering off.

An hour later, the trucker was about to leave. He grabbed the waiter once more.

"Are you positive there's no women around here?"

"I'm positive," said the waiter. "But you can still fuck old Wong the Chinaman if you want to."

"I told you I don't go for none of that shit," grumbled the trucker. He opened the door to leave. Slowly, he turned back to the waiter. "But if I did want to fuck old Wong the Chinaman, how much would it cost me?"

"Ten bucks."

"Ten bucks to fuck a Chinaman?"

"Why, shit," answered the waiter, "ten bucks is just for me and my brother Bob to hold old Wong down. He don't go for that shit, either!"

♦

What's green and flies around Greenwich Village?

Peter Pansy.

♦

Two teamsters were working on the dock. One turned to the other and said, "Did you know there's a homo working in the crew?"
"No," his friend replied. "Who is he?"
"I can't tell you that!"
"Oh, come on!"
"You have to kiss me first."

♦

What do you call a woman with her tongue sticking out?

A lesbian with a hard-on.

♦

What do you call a gay Indian?

A brave fucker.

♦

Did you hear about the gay pope?

He couldn't decide if he was divine or just gorgeous.

Racial Mixtures

What's three miles long, green, and has a black dot in the front?

Next year's Saint Patrick's Day parade in Chicago.

◆

What's the difference between a Pole and a black?

The black takes the dishes out of the sink before he pisses in it.

◆

Why can't you circumcise an Iranian?

Because there's no end to those pricks.

◆

Did you hear about the new German microwave oven?

It seats six.

◆

A Texas businessman arrives at his hotel in the heart of a major Japanese city. He arranges to have a beautiful Japanese prostitute be his companion for the night.

The woman arrives, and is more beautiful and sensual than he had imagined; once in bed he takes her with great enthusiasm and unbridled lust. During the act he hears his partner cry out many times, "Sung wha! Sung wha!"

"That must be Japanese for 'terrific,'" thinks the Texan, "because I can tell from the way she's thrashing around she's never been had like this before."

The next morning, the Texan has an appointment with two very important Japanese business associates to play golf. Naturally he wants to impress the men with his friendliness and goodwill, so when the older gentleman makes a hole in one, the Texan shouts, "Sung wha! Sung wha!"

The Japanese turns, eyebrows raised in surprise. "Wrong hole? What you mean, wrong hole?"

♦

What do you call a Mexican baptism?

Bean dip.

♦

Did you hear about the queer Irishman?

He liked women better than whiskey.

♦

A Pole walks into a travel agency and says to the agent behind the counter, "I'd like to take the one hundred dollar Trip to Nowhere."

The agent takes the Pole's money, hands him a ticket, and hits him over the head with a blackjack. He then drags the unconscious Pole into the back room.

About fifteen minutes later an Italian walks in and requests a ticket for the one hundred dollar Trip to Nowhere. Again, the agent takes the money, gives the man a ticket, hits him over the head, and drags him into the back room.

Several hours later the Italian and the Pole wake up in a rowboat in the middle of the Pacific Ocean. The Italian looks around and says to his companion, "Gee, I wonder if they serve drinks on this lousy trip."

"They didn't last year," replies the Pole.

◆

How do you get twenty Cubans in a paper cup?

Tell them it floats.

◆

Why don't they kill the flies in Puerto Rico?

Because they're the national bird.

◆

The Frenchman at the beach was surrounded by beautiful women. He was watched enviously by a Pole sitting all alone.

When the Frenchman got up to get a drink, the Pole followed him.

"Excuse me, sir," the Pole said, "but I couldn't help noticing how women are attracted to you. Would you mind revealing your secret?"

Smiling, the Frenchman said, "It's simple. I put a potato in my bathing suit. It drives the women wild."

"Thanks, I'll try it," said the Pole, and he hurried away.

Three days later the Pole again met the Frenchman at the beach.

"Hey! I thought you said that if I put a potato in my bathing suit it would drive the women wild. I've had one there for three days and women are going out of their way to avoid me!"

The Frenchman eyed the Pole and said, "Try putting it in the front."

♦

What do you call a white man in a Cadillac?

White Power.

A black man in a Cadillac?

Black Power.

A Puerto Rican in a Cadillac?

Grand theft, auto.

♦

What's this?

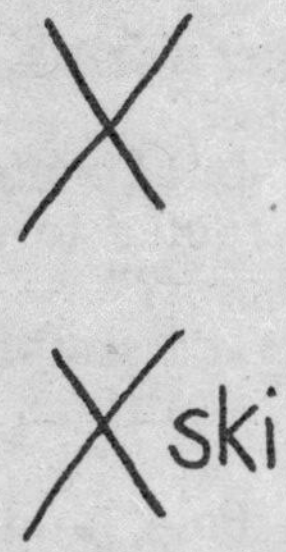

A Pole cosigning a loan for a black man.

♦

Have you heard about the new French-African restaurant?

It's called Chez What?

♦

Why do they call camels the ships of the desert?

Because they're full of Iranian semen.

♦

Three foreign legionnaires—a Jew, an Italian, and a Pole—were to be flogged for disobeying orders. Their sergeant, not wishing to be unnecessarily cruel, asked each man if they wanted anything put on their backs to help them bear their punishment.

The Italian requested olive oil. It was applied to his skin, and he was whipped within an inch of his life.

The Pole said, "I am strong like bull. I need nothing." He too was whipped unmercifully, but didn't utter a sound.

The Jew, who had witnessed both whippings, was then asked what he wanted on his back. After a minute of thought he replied, "The Pole."

♦

Why don't Puerto Ricans have checking accounts?

Because it's hard to sign checks with a spray can.

♦

What do you call an abortion in Czechoslovakia?

A canceled czech.

♦

Did you hear about the new Mexican war movie?

It's called Tacolipsnow.

♦

An American vacationing in Spain goes into a restaurant near the bullring. He doesn't know enough of the language to read the menu, but notices that the man at the next table is being served an extraordinary dish. The waiter has lifted a large silver dome to reveal two big beefy filets smothered in sautéed onions and an exquisite sauce.

The American calls the waiter over and asks what the dish is.

"It is the house speciality, *señor*," the waiter replies.

"Fine, I'll have that."

"I am very sorry, *señor*, but there is only one portion prepared each day. If you like, we can reserve tomorrow's portion for you. The bullfight is over at three; you may come for dinner any time after four."

The American reserves his dinner and leaves.

The next day he returns after four, as specified, and requests the house speciality. The waiter brings out a silver-domed platter and lifts the cover, revealing a dish full of sautéed onions, the same exquisite sauce, and two small round nuggets of meat. Furious, the American says to the waiter, "This isn't the same dish you served yesterday! What happened to those huge filets?"

"Many pardons, *señor*," the waiter says, "but sometimes the bull wins."

◆

What do you get when you cross a Jew and a gypsy?

A chain of empty stores.

◆

What's the difference between an Irish wedding and an Irish funeral?

One less drunk.

◆

Why don't Cubans like to take baths?

They'd rather wash up on shore.

◆

What's a Puerto Rican American Express Card?

A knife.

◆

Did you hear about the family of nine Puerto Ricans who moved out of the outhouse?

It seems the Mexicans upstairs were making too much noise.

♦

What's Greek foreplay?

Here, sheepie, sheepie, sheepie.

♦

Why don't Mexicans barbecue?

Because the beans slip through the grill.

♦

What's the German word for "bra"?

Stopemfromfloppen

♦

Why did the Greek boy leave his homeland?

He didn't like the way he was being reared.

And why did he return?

He couldn't leave his brother's behind.

♦

What was the motto of the Greeks who fought in the Falkland Islands War?

Save the sheep.

Can you name the three most dangerous people in New York?

A Pole with an idea.
A Jew with a lawyer.
A gay with a chipped front tooth.

During the French Revolution, three men were sentenced to the guillotine. One was a Frenchman, one was an Englishman, and the third was a Pole.

The Frenchman takes his place on the block and the blade is released. On the way down, it jams. Traditionally, if the guillotine fails, the condemned man is pardoned. So the Frenchman is set free.

Seeing this happen strikes a spark of hope in the two remaining prisoners. The Englishman takes his place at the guillotine. Again the machine malfunctions and the Englishman is set free.

Now it's the Pole's turn. But as he is being led to the platform he begins to struggle and scream. "I ain't going near that thing until you get it fixed!"

How do Germans tie their shoes?

In Nazis.

If you have enjoyed *Outrageously Offensive Jokes*, I recommend the following titles for your reading enjoyment:

THE LIONS, Claude Balls
THE YELLOW RIVER, I. P. Daily
OPEN KIMONO, Seymour Hair
FRENCH RUPTURE, Jacques Tutite
CHINESE HERNIA, Huan Hung Lo
THE HAWAIIAN RAPE, Kamanawanna Laya
THE MAN IN THE BUSH, Izzy Nude
THE POLISH MILKMAN, I. Pultitsky
RUSSIAN CASTRATORS IN HISTORY, I. Cutchakokoff
GO TO HELL, Hugo First
I FELL OFF MT. EVEREST, Eileen Dover
HIT BELOW THE BELT, Lord Howard Hertz
THE CUNNING LINGUIST, Hugh Lickeroff
UNUSUAL CHINESE WALLPAPERS, Huo Flung Dung
THE PHILOSOPHY OF SEX, Ophelia Kant
PROTOSCOPY AND ASTROLOGY, Dr. Uranus
NEW WAYS TO TAN: THE FAR EASTERN METHOD, Hoo Shatan-U
THE NEW FEMININE HYGIENE, Honey Uptwat
THE MARQUISE DE SADE REVISITED, Bruce Menbeetem
HOW TO FIND THE PERFECT JAP WIFE, I. Weindendeined